Weather, Wind, and Kite Strings

Ron Benson

Lynn Bryan

Kim Newlove

Charolette Player

Liz Stenson

CONSULTANTS

Susan Elliott

Diane Lomond

Ken MacInnis

Elizabeth Parchment

PRENTICE HALL GINN CANADA

Contents

Bibliography

 Selections with this symbol are available on audio.

 This symbol indicates student writing.

Canadian selections are marked with this symbol.

Aska's Seasons

by Warabé Aska
Poetry selected by Alberto Manguel

Winter

Snowbirds

A pure white feather floats down.
Oh, at that moment
We both hope that happiness
May also be like a white bird,
Quietly descending.

Lin Ling

Ring-Around

Round the green gravel the grass is so green,
And all the fine ladies that ever were seen;
Washed in milk and dressed in silk,
The last shall marry the love of her dream.

Anonymous

The Puppeteers

Ceaseless wanderers from of old, the puppeteers,
Over all the earth searching ever a new home.
They pitch their tents and sing
in the night to the mountain moon.

Fujiwara no Tadamachi

Wind
The star, like a cat, turns in the windy sky.
You! fly, if you can, among the autumn trees!

Alfonsina Storni

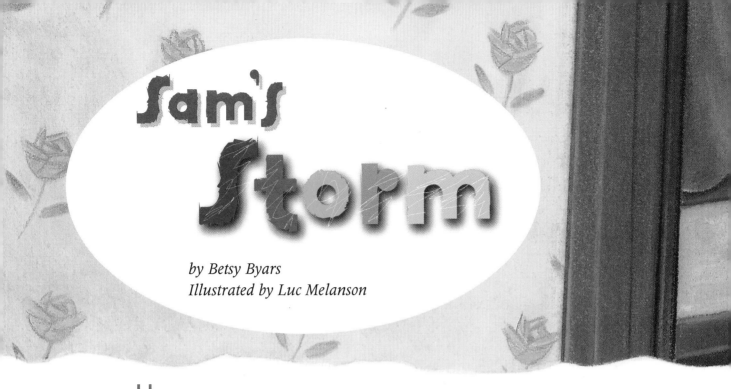

Sam's Storm

by Betsy Byars
Illustrated by Luc Melanson

"**I** am in pain!" Sam yelled at the top of his lungs.

There was no answer.

"I am in great pain!"

Again, no answer. The only sound in the big empty house was Sam's sigh.

He looked down at his red, swollen feet, propped on pillows. He realized that he now knew the exact meaning of the word "throb." His feet throbbed. He had five hornet stings on one and four on the other. And they throbbed.

"I am in pain and agony!" he yelled, even though there was no one to hear him. The entire family had gone in the pickup truck to see a thirty-five-kilogram snapping turtle Mr. Johnson had pulled out of his fishing pond.

He had watched them drive away, his cousins in the back of the truck, laughing and excited, his grandparents in the front.

"You're sure you don't mind being left alone?" his grandmother had asked.

"I don't mind," he had answered, in a way that should have let her know he minded a lot.

"We'll be back in less than an hour."

"Don't worry about me."

"Here's some lemonade and cookies if you get hungry. Here are two aspirins in case your feet hurt."

In case they hurt! he had wanted to yell. What do you think they've been doing all day? I am in agony!

"This is the Johnsons' phone number, where we'll be, and the phone's right here at your elbow. We'll be back before the thunderstorms."

Every afternoon since he'd been at his grandparents' farm, they had had thunderstorms—big, powerful storms with booming thunder and streaks of lightning. The only one who hated the storms more than Sam was his grandparents' big black dog, Bull.

"Now, you're sure you—"

"I'll be fine!"

Actually, it was amazing how little sympathy he was getting. His feet were as big as balloons. His toes were like sausages. Each hornet sting was a white welt in the red, swollen flesh.

And yet, because it was his own fault, because he had gone out in the yard barefoot, nobody seemed to care. How was he to know hornets made nests in the ground? How was he to know he could be stung, and that, while he was hopping in fear and pain from one foot to the other, he could be stung eight more times?

His cousins had known, but they were farm kids. He was from the city. He thought hornets only made nests in trees. His eyes filled with tears of sympathy for himself.

He heard scratching at the screen door. "Bull?" he called. "Is that you?"

The only time Bull ever wanted to come into the house was when a storm was coming. Bull, his grandfather said, was better than the weatherman at predicting storms.

"When that dog wants in the house, you can bet a storm's coming. And the more he wants in, the worse the storm's going to be. Just before the '84 tornado, he came *through* the screen door."

"Why is he so afraid of storms?" Sam had asked.

"He blew in here one night during a storm. That's the way we got him. We went out one morning, and the yard was covered with limbs and wood, buckets and stray chickens, every kind of thing. And under the front steps was Bull. Since that day, he hasn't been able to abide a storm."

"Didn't you try to find out who he belonged to?"

"We asked around. But if a dog gets blown away in a storm like that, he can't ever find his way home. He gets disoriented. He could live a kilometre away, and he still wouldn't be able to find it."

Bull barked at the front door.

"I'd let you in," Sam called, "but I'm in agony!"

Sam glanced out the window. To the east the sky was bright blue, the clouds white.

"Anyway, there's no storm in sight, Bull," he called.

Bull was not comforted. He barked again and scratched at the screen. Sam rested his head against the back of the chair. He looked at the phone. Now would be a good time to call his parents and tell them about his feet. He had the number of their hotel in San Francisco. Maybe he could pretend to be calling to see if they were having fun, and then just mention casually that he had stepped on nine hornets and . . .

Bull's face appeared in the window. For a huge, strong dog—that was how he got the name Bull—he could look terrified. His tongue was lolling out of his mouth, drops of saliva were dropping onto the sill, his eyes bulged, his whole body trembled.

At that moment a long, low rumble of thunder came from the west. Bull threw back his head and howled.

Suddenly Sam was uneasy, too. Maybe, he thought, I am sitting here looking at this patch of blue sky, thinking there is no danger, while behind me . . .

He glanced quickly over his shoulder. Through the hall, he could see the edge of the dining-room window. The sky there was black.

He turned and met Bull's pleading eyes. "Stop looking at me like that. I can't do anything."

Bull barked twice, the last bark ending in a howl.

"I'm telling you, I'm helpless." He broke off to listen to the newest roll of thunder. The sound was moving closer. This storm was coming faster than usual.

"Now you're making me nervous," he told Bull.

The dog put his huge paws against the screen and began to dig. Slits opened in the screen. There was another roll of thunder. Bull dug faster.

"Stop it!" Sam yelled. But Bull was beyond hearing a command.

The slits in the screen were lengthening. Soon the screen was in ribbons. Bull began to pry his way through. He jumped in, hit the floor, and without pausing ran for the chair where Sam sat.

"No!" Sam yelled, holding out his arms to protect himself. He recalled that Bull had jumped onto his grandfather's lap the afternoon before. "Look at my big baby," his grandfather had said.

"No!"

In one leap, Bull cleared the footstool and was on Sam's lap. The pain jarred Sam's feet. Tears came to his eyes. "Get down!" he moaned, but Bull was curled into a ball of fear. His soft, pleading eyes looked up at Sam.

With a sigh, Sam gave in. Getting Bull off his lap would be more painful than letting him stay. "All right, but be still."

Actually, it was comforting to have the big dog on his lap. He

rested his arms on Bull's trembling shoulders. "I know how you feel, pal, because I don't care for storms either."

There was another crash of thunder. This time the sound echoed from cloud to cloud, as if it were building force. Bull tried to bury his head under Sam's arm.

At that moment, wind swept through the house, blowing through the open windows. Upstairs, a door slammed. On the porch, the hanging baskets of plants began hitting the rail. The curtains were drawn tight against the screens.

Sam picked up the phone. He was going to call the Johnsons. He looked for the number, but it had blown across the room in the first rush of wind.

"Why don't they come home?" he asked. "Don't they see the storm? How long does it take to look at a turtle?"

The wind at his neck had stiffened. Outside, branches blew against the house. A chair on the porch turned over with a bang. The porch swing crashed against the house.

"We ought to go to the basement," he said. Every afternoon his grandmother listened to the storm, judged it, and said, "Well, it's not bad enough for us to go to the basement."

"This one," he told Bull, "is bad enough for us to go to the basement."

Turning sideways, he dumped Bull on the floor. Bull waited in a crouch, tail between his huge legs, ears flat. Then he crawled under the nearest table.

Sam slipped off the chair and landed hard on his knees. He too waited, crouched in pain. Slowly, he straightened.

"Come on," he told Bull. The dog only trembled harder.

Sam crossed the room, grimacing with pain, and grabbed Bull's thick collar. "Come on."

Bull pulled back, bracing himself, not wanting to leave the safety of the table. "Come on!" The floor was slick and well waxed, and Bull slid out. Sam dragged him into the hall.

Through the front door, Sam saw the blackest sky he had ever seen in his life. Drops of water the size of marbles began to pelt the porch. The old oak tree groaned in the wind.

Sam struggled down the hall, dragging Bull with him over the slick floor. Outside, an oak limb crashed against the house. Glass shattered.

At last Sam's hand closed around the knob to the basement door.

He pulled, and in a rush Bull slipped past him, down the steps, and behind the water heater. "Thanks for waiting," Sam said.

He crawled down two steps, and the wind slammed the door behind him. He was in darkness now. He felt his way down the stairs, step by step, like a small child. As he got to the bottom, he heard a noise overhead, a crash so loud it seemed the whole world had been split apart. He covered his head with his hands and waited for the worst.

"Sam!"

He lifted his head

"Sam?"

"I'm in the basement." He had no idea how long he had been here, waiting out the storm—maybe an hour.

The basement door opened, and Sam looked up at his grandfather. "Are you all right, Sam?"

"Yes."

Behind his grandfather there was no hall, mirror, or rose wallpaper. Behind his grandfather was a solid wall of leaves. "What happened?"

"The oak tree," his grandfather said, choking on the words, unable to continue.

Sam began to climb the stairs on his knees. On the top step, he stopped. There was no way to get through the hall.

"The living room," his grandfather said, pointing helplessly. "I thought you—" Again he had to stop.

Sam was stunned. He said, "The tree fell on the living room? What's grandma going to say. She loved that tree. She loved this house."

His grandfather shook his head.

"It can be fixed, can't it?"

"Maybe."

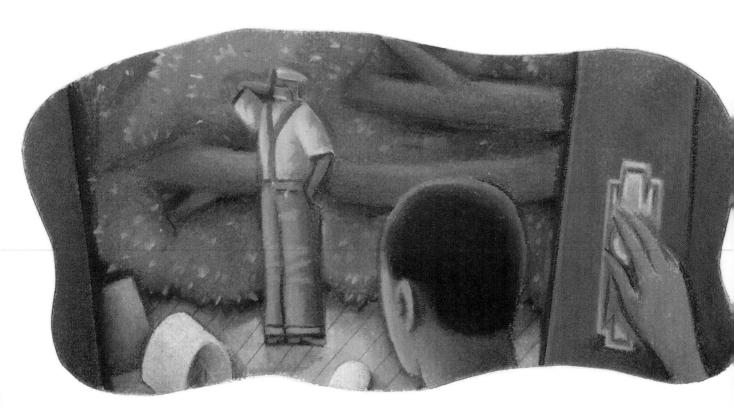

Sam heard a noise on the stairs, and he looked down. Bull was coming up. As the big dog squeezed past, Sam scratched him behind the ears. Bull disappeared into the branches.

"We'd better let your grandma know you're safe," his grandfather said. "You're what she's worried about."

"I'm fine." When he said it this time, it was true.

"Will you be all right till I get back? I have to walk. Trees are down all over the road."

Sam nodded. His grandfather went to the kitchen door and stood for a moment, hunched over like an old man, looking at the ruins. Keeping to the wall, Sam took slow, painful steps on his swollen feet. He paused beside his grandfather at the kitchen door.

From here he could see the damage. The huge oak tree had split the side of the house and crushed the room where he had sat nursing his swollen feet.

He held onto the door to steady himself. He felt disoriented. Like Bull, he could never get back to the place where he had sat an hour before, yelling, "I am in pain."

Bull was running around the tree, sniffing the broken branches, leaping over the leaves, wild with excitement. The huge ball of roots and dirt was as high as the porch roof.

"One thing," his grandfather said. "You probably saved old Bull's life."

Sam hesitated and then said, truthfully, "We saved each other."

His grandfather nodded, squared his shoulders, and went down the steps.

ABOUT THE

AUTHOR   BETSY BYARS

Betsy Byars grew up in Charlotte, North Carolina. In the 1950s she began writing articles for *The Saturday Evening Post*, *Look*, and other magazines. Since then she has written over a dozen books, including *The Summer of the Swans*, *Cracker Jackson*, *My Brother Ant*, and *Dead Letter*. Her award-winning books have been translated into nine languages. She says, "Making up stories and characters is so interesting that I'm never bored. Each book has been a different writing experience. . . ." Betsy Byars is also a pilot, and lives on an air strip in South Carolina. She has four grown children and seven grandchildren.

Weather Whys

by Valerie Wyatt

Why are rain clouds so dark? How acid is acid rain? Who is Jack Frost? Read on for the answers to these and other weather whys, whats, whos, and hows.

Illustrated by Dan Hobbs

Q. What's a weather map?

A. It's a map that shows the main high and low pressure areas across the country and the cold and warm fronts. The weather map in your local paper might look like the one below. H stands for a high-pressure area, which generally means good weather; L stands for a low-pressure area, which often spells bad weather. The fronts (the edges of warm or cold air masses) are marked like this:

WARM FRONT   **COLD FRONT**

Some weather maps use symbols to give other information. Here are some of the international weather symbols. If you don't find them on the weather map in your newspaper, try marking them on yourself.

THUNDERSTORM		HAZE
LIGHTNING		DRIZZLE
FREEZING RAIN		RAIN
SNOW		SHOWERS

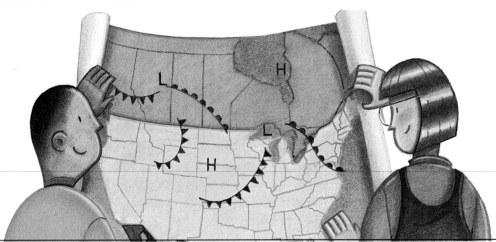

Weather maps can tell you what kind of weather to expect. Weather moves from west to east. So if you want to know what kind of weather is on its way, look at what's happening on the map west of where you live.

Q. What is wind chill?

A. Ever noticed how you feel colder when the wind blows? That's because the wind blows away a thin layer of warm air that usually surrounds your body. On windless days this layer of air acts like insulation in a house and helps to keep you warm; on windy days—whoosh!—it's whipped away and you lose body heat.

A scientist named Paul Siple came up with a way of figuring out just how much colder you would feel with various speeds of wind. For example, if the thermometer said it was −18°C and the wind was blowing at 16 km/h, he calculated that it would feel more like −30°C. He called this wind chill. Today weather forecasters often announce the wind chill so that people will know how to dress for the cold.

Q. How acid is acid rain?

A. You don't need to worry about its eating holes in your umbrella. It's not that acidic. But acid rain that falls into lakes can harm the lakes and kill the fish.

The acidity of rain is measured by its pH level. Pure rain has a pH level of 5.6.

Acid rain is any rain with a pH level *lower* than 5.6.

If too much acid rain falls into a lake, the lake may become acidified. You can see what happens to the fish as the pH level drops. Fish cannot survive with a pH level below 4.5.

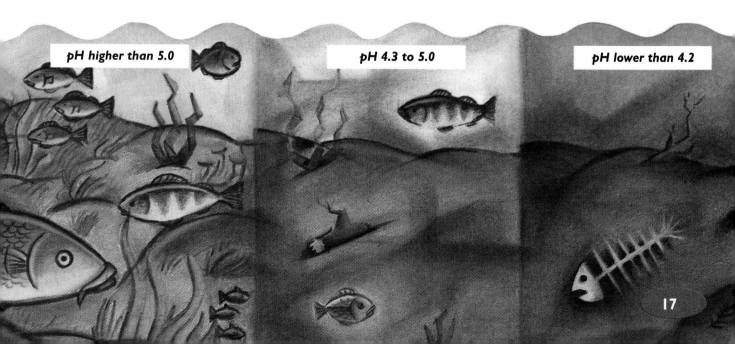

pH higher than 5.0

pH 4.3 to 5.0

pH lower than 4.2

Q. What's a chinook?

A. It's a hot dry wind that can turn winter into summer in a matter of minutes. One blustery cold winter day in 1943, the townspeople of Rapid City, South Dakota, went from snowsuits to shorts in just fifteen minutes as a sudden chinook boosted the town's temperature from −12°C to 13°C.

Where does such a hot dry wind come from? A moisture-laden wind flows up one side of a mountain and dumps its moisture. The now-dry wind warms as it flows down the other side of the mountain.

The chinook got its name from an Aboriginal word meaning snow-eater. No wonder. A chinook wind can "eat" a knee-deep snowfall overnight. That sure beats shovelling the stuff.

Q. What's El Niño?

A. It's a warming of the ocean's surface that happens around Christmas every year off the coast of Ecuador and Peru. Some years it's hardly noticeable. But other years, El Niño turns the world's weather upside down. Places that are normally sunny and dry, such as Florida, are drenched with rainstorms. Countries expecting a much-needed rainy season, such as Indonesia, have a drought. All of this happens because the warm ocean water of El Niño starts a chain reaction in the atmosphere and shakes up the normal weather patterns.

Q. Why are rain clouds so dark?

A. Because they're loaded with ice crystals, cloud droplets, and rain droplets that are about to fall. The droplets and crystals block the sunlight from coming through the cloud. The more droplets and crystals, the less light that gets through, and the darker the cloud looks. Really dark clouds contain a lot of snow, which blocks the light even more.

Q. Who is Jack Frost?

A. Jack Frost came from a pretty cool family. His father was a Scandinavian wind god named Kari. Jack himself had a son named Snjo, or Snow in English.

It was Jack's job to decorate the world with frost in winter. He did this fairly well for hundreds of years until (horrors!) the real story of frost was discovered by scientists. Jack was out of a job.

You can make frost just as Jack Frost did.

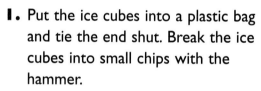

You'll need:
- ice cubes
- a plastic bag
- a hammer
- an empty tin can
- salt

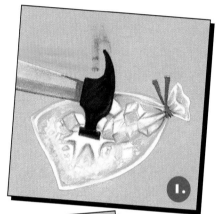

1. Put the ice cubes into a plastic bag and tie the end shut. Break the ice cubes into small chips with the hammer.

2. Put a layer of ice in the tin can about 3 cm thick, then a thin layer of salt, another layer of ice, and so on until the can is full.

3. Watch what forms. If it's a dry day, with not much humidity in the air, you may have to breathe on the outside of the can to produce frost.

What happened? When moist air hits the cold surface of the can, the water in it freezes and sticks to the can. The result is frost. This process of going from a gas (your breath) to a solid (frost) is called sublimation. It's what happens when frost forms in winter.

Q. Can you smell rain before it falls?
A. Some scientists think you can. They believe that plants give off more scent when the air is moist, before a rainfall. When people smell these scents, they have learned to expect rain.

Other scientists believe it's all in your nose. They say the moisture in the air tickles your sense of smell and makes it more sensitive. Try this for yourself. Compare how strong a lemon smells in a misty bathroom and in a dry room.

Q. Is it true that no two snowflakes are alike?
A. That's what people have believed for a long time. And for good reason. To be identical, two snowflakes would have to fall through *exactly* the same conditions. The tiniest extra bit of moisture or the smallest puff of wind will make two flakes look different.

Identical snowflakes seemed impossible—until physicist Nancy Wright caught two look-alikes when she was collecting snowflake samples in the winter of 1988. She took pictures of the snowflakes and enlarged them. To the naked eye, they appear to be identical. But even so, Nancy Wright isn't convinced. She says there may be differences that are so tiny you can't spot them.

ABOUT THE AUTHOR — VALERIE WYATT

Valerie Wyatt is the author of four books about science for kids, including *Weatherwatch* and *The Science Book for Girls and Other Intelligent Beings*. She was the managing editor of *Owl* magazine for four years and currently is the senior editor of non-fiction books at Kids Can Press. Valerie lives in Victoria, BC.

Dogs' Paws and Diamond Dust

A Canadian Weather Almanac

Illustrated by Philippe Germaine

Records, proverbs, recipes, and more!

Watch That Weather Forecast!

Weather can affect your health! Here are some items to watch for in a weather forecast.

- **Wind chill factor.** In winter, this tells you how dangerous or uncomfortable the cold, windy conditions can be.
- **Humidex.** In summer, this warns you about hot, muggy weather.
- **UV index.** This warns you when ultraviolet rays may harm your skin.
- **Air quality index.** This tells you when there will be a lot of pollution in the air.

The Why of Weather Proverbs

What will the weather do next? Here are some handy sayings, and why they work—most of the time!

**Red sky at night, sailor's delight;
Red sky in the morning, sailors take warning.**

When the sky looks red at night, it's because bits of dust are hanging low in the air at sunset, reflecting the sun's rays. Dust only stays low like this when cool heavy air keeps it close to the ground—and cool heavy air usually means fine weather the next day. So when the evening sky is red, sailors can count on safe weather at sea.

The second part of the rhyme has a different explanation. When the sky looks red in the morning it's because the sun's light is reflected off drops of water in the air. Moisture in the air means clouds will form and rain will soon follow. So a red morning sky warns sailors at sea to be careful.

**A ring around the sun or moon
Brings rain or snow upon you soon.**

When wind pushes water drops high into the air, they freeze into tiny bits of ice. When the rays of the sun or moon shine on these icy bits, a ring appears. It's a sure sign that lots of moisture is building up high in the air, and a lot of rain or snow is coming.

**Mackerel sky and mares' tails
Grab your hat and lower the sails!**

High, wispy clouds shaped like fish scales or horses' tails are the first sign that a lot of warm wet air is rising over cooler drier air. Almost always, wind and rain will follow soon.

Strange Showers

Stay home during these downpours!

- Live lizards fell on Montreal, Quebec.

- Tiny beetles fell on Rock Candy Creek, British Columbia.

- Green toads rained from the sky in Belleville, Ontario, and brown ants came down in Winnipeg, Manitoba.

- A shower of fish fell on Moosejaw, Saskatchewan. In Toronto, Ontario, a single fish fell out of the sky. It bounced off a man's face and swam away down a flooded gutter!

Cold Weather Pet Tip

When it's really cold, put petroleum jelly on your dog's paws before taking it for a walk.

Canadian Weather Records

The wettest place in Canada is Henderson Lake, on Vancouver Island. It has an average annual rainfall of 6655 mm. Henderson Lake also received the greatest precipitation in one year— 8122.4 mm in 1931.

Canada's highest maximum air temperature was registered in Midale and Yellowgrass, Saskatchewan, on July 5, 1937. It was 45.0°C.

The lowest minimum air temperature ever recorded in Canada was at Snag, Yukon Territory, on February 3, 1947. The temperature fell to –63°C.

Canada's heaviest hailstone fell on Cedoux, Saskatchewan, on August 27, 1973. It had a mass of 290 g.

The highest wind speed for one hour in Canada was recorded at Quaqtaq, Quebec, on November 18, 1931. The wind blew at 201.1 km/h.

The record for highest average hours of fog annually is 1890 hours. It's held by Argentia, Newfoundland.

Ontario has more thunderstorms than any other province. Thunderstorms occur there on an average of 34 days a year.

• • • • • •

Winter Weather Folklore

Birch trees lose some bark each fall, but if they lose a lot, it will be a mild winter.

If the black bands on a woolly bear caterpillar are close together, with not much brown in between, it will be a cold winter.

If muskrats build low nests, winter will be warm. If they build taller, higher nests, there will be plenty of snow.

Heavy crops of berries on the mountain ash, or heavy loads of cones on evergreens, mean a cold winter.

Big Blows!

Hang onto your hat if you're ever caught in one of these!

Barber: a powerful wind blowing snow that freezes on hair and beards

Chinook: a warm dry wind that blows down the eastern slopes of the Rocky Mountains in Alberta

Plow Wind: a fierce wind that blows down from squall lines and thunderstorms in Saskatchewan

Suete: a strong southeast gale blowing along the coast of Cape Breton Island, Nova Scotia

Wreckhouse Effect: a violent wind that blows in western Newfoundland

Yoho Blow: a strong cold wind in the Yoho Valley, in British Columbia

Weather Whoppers

Thick fog? The Bay of Fundy's the best place for that. Why, it gets so thick you can sit on the boat rail and lean your back against it. You've got to be careful, though. If the fog lifts, you could fall overboard!

Did you hear about the farmer who drove his sleigh to town in a chinook? Driving his horse at a gallop, he just kept the front of the runners on the snow. The back ones were dragging in the mud. When they got to town, the farmer had frostbite. His wife was sitting in the back of the sleigh, and she had heatstroke!

How dry does it get in an Alberta drought? Well, there was one rancher whose dog dried out so much he had to wheel it around in a wheelbarrow to bark at the cows!

WAF!

Home Remedy

Got a cold? Try taking blackcurrant tea. To make some, put one heaping teaspoon of blackcurrant preserves into a glass of hot water. Stir and drink. It's guaranteed to taste good, and the Vitamin C in it might even help you feel better!

Rainbows are always on the opposite side of the sky from the sun.

Thirty-six percent of Canada's yearly precipitation falls in the form of snow.

The first electronic computer to be used for weather forecasting was named **MANIAC**.

Lightning can travel at a speed of 140 000 km per second.

The seven years with the warmest *global* temperatures ever recorded are all since 1980. In order of the warmest, they are: 1990, 1988, 1991, 1987, 1983, 1989, 1981.

When it's very, very cold, tiny water droplets sometimes freeze in the air and drift down very slowly. Because of the way they sparkle, they are called diamond dust.

How Long Are the Seasons?

The dates of the seasons can vary from year to year. This is because our calendar is not exact, and the Earth's orbit varies slightly.

The current lengths of the seasons in the Northern Hemisphere are:

Summer: 93.641 days
Autumn: 89.834 days
Winter: 88.994 days
Spring: 92.771 days

Great Canadian Weather Mystery!

The Year Without a Summer happened in eastern North America in 1816. In Quebec and the Maritime provinces, there was snow on the ground in June, and repeated frosts until September. Crops died, and in some places people went hungry.

What caused it? Some scientists blame the eruption of the volcano Tambora in Indonesia in 1815. Dust and ash from the eruption may have blocked the sun's rays and cooled the world's weather. Others think sunspots might be to blame. The Year Without a Summer remains a great weather mystery.

Lost in a Blizzard

My family was travelling in the countryside when it started to snow hard. My brother Jay said, "Look over there. It's a cave! Let's go in for shelter!"

We took our flashlights, lanterns, and shovels out of the car and went to the cave. After we got in the cave it started snowing so hard that it covered the cave doorway. We were trapped! We had our shovels, except that we couldn't get out. We went looking for another doorway but had to be careful of the pit. We were throwing rocks ahead of us until we found it. The pit wasn't as deep as we expected, except we needed more and more rocks.

We heard little pellets landing on the roof. We went back to the entrance and tried to get out, but the pellets were ice pellets and we were trapped even more. For hours we were walking around looking for other entrances that we could escape through, but they were all buried.

We walked around until we came to the first entrance. Then I got an idea to put rocks around a fire and use our shovels to throw the hot rocks into the snow to melt it. We found some sticks and used our lanterns to light the fire. My idea worked and we were saved! After that we never drove around the countryside in the winter.

Benjamin Shaw
Age 9

I like to write because I can be creative and use my imagination freely. When I write stories, I enjoy being able to make certain things happen that I know are impossible in real life.

Benjamin Shaw

Spring

Sun hot as fire
Clouds soft as cotton
Flowers like your mother's perfume
Rain makes the earth smell like ice cream
Raspberries taste like the earth
Butterflies flit in the wind.

Thunder hard as rock
Brown mud like a bear
The breeze warm like a cozy bed
Frogs green as the grass
Birds singing like a choir

That's spring.

Trishia McDonald and Starniss Boulanger
Age 10

Dear Mother Nature

How are you? I am fine. I think you are very interesting because you have the power to create new creatures and you have the power to keep the ecosystem alive. You have the special ability to make something dead into something new, like when trees lose their leaves in the fall, new leaves come in the spring.

When I think of all the creatures in the world, I say to myself that if there weren't any leaves, water, plants, and food we would not be alive. I just wrote this letter to you so that you know that I thank you.

Sincerely,
Zach

Zach DesRoches
Age 12

Seasons

There are four different seasons, which are summer, fall, winter, spring. I like summer best of all—the days are very hot. Temperatures go up to about 32 degrees and the nights are warm. The grass is green and the flowers of many colors are beautiful. The trees are full of green leaves. The birds are flying and singing.

The next season is fall, when the temperature is around 18 degrees. The leaves start turning different colors and fall off. The days turn cloudy and nights cool. The green grass and the flowers start to die. The birds start to go south for winter.

The next season is winter. It is when sometimes the temperature drops down to about 0 degrees. The trees are dead. The days and nights are very cold. The white snow falls to the ground and all the animals go to find a home until next spring. It is when you can go skating and tobogganing.

The next season is spring. Spring is when animals come out and the birds come back. The flowers bloom, and the trees and the grass come back to life. The days and nights become a bit warmer. But for me I still like summer best.

Stephanie Hill
Age 12

> I did my best on this project and I hope it can be useful to other students. If you want to do a project on any topic, the word I want you to think of is "Research."

Nurgis Maroof

Lightning

Lightning is very fast. The flash of lightning reaches us much before the sound. This is because light travels much faster than sound.

When it flashes, a bright streak is drawn in the clouds. This streak is either between two clouds or between the clouds and the earth. When it streaks, electricity flows through the air towards the earth. When two charged clouds approach each other, there is a flash of lightning. This flash can be as long as fifty kilometres.

The lightning produced between the earth and clouds is dangerous for high buildings. In order to protect these buildings from lightning, pointed metallic rods are fixed to the roof. The lightning strikes the tops of these rods and it is taken through the walls, down to the earth, and buried inside. They are called lightning conductors. Buildings fitted with these conductors cannot be damaged by lightning.

Nurgis Maroof
Grade 5/6

Hawks Flying South for the Winter

by David M. Bird

Every fall like clockwork, as you're settling into a new school year, thousands of hawks across Canada are flying south to their winter homes. How do they get there? How long will it take them? Why don't you join these birds of prey on their journey and find out.

Hawks are hunting birds, or raptors. They have hooked beaks, sharp talons (claws), and keen eyesight. Some of them have very broad wings that help them soar for very long distances. These birds leave their summer breeding grounds because the insects, mice, and small birds they feed on are not easily found when the ground is covered with ice and snow.

Do I Have to Go?

Although most soaring hawks migrate, a few individual birds will stay behind if they think they've found a good source of food and shelter.

Are We There Yet?

Some species, or kinds, of hawks, such as the ferruginous (feh-ROO-jeh-nes) hawk, travel several hundred kilometres south into the United States. They can usually get there in just a few days.

Other hawks, such as the broad-winged species, will fly, soar, and glide as far south as Central America, taking a couple of weeks to reach their destination.

But the most well travelled of all these birds has to be the Swainson's hawk. To get to its distant home on the bottom tip of South America, a Swainson's hawk will have to fly as many as 13 000 kilometres. That's like crossing Canada from coast to coast and back again! The Swainson's hawk can reach its destination in about four or five weeks, stopping every night to rest.

A Swainson's hawk.

Getting There Is Half the Fun

Because of their broad wings, hawks migrate by soaring in the sky in lazy circles—a lot like the way a hang-glider uses thermals, or warm air currents, to rise high into the air and then glide. Thermals are created when warm air rises straight up over flat land. Hawks will fly close to mountains or shoreline cliffs because of the way the air moves up when it hits the sides of these landforms.

By riding these currents, hawks don't have to flap their wings as often as other birds. They'll climb as high as possible and then glide down just in time to catch the next thermal. Then the cycle starts all over again. Kind of like a wind-powered roller coaster.

How High Is High?

Most raptors fly only 200 to 1000 metres above the ground. Broad-winged hawks and Swainson's hawks can fly a lot higher. They've been detected by radar as far up as 6400 metres. That's almost as high as the cruising altitude of some airplanes!

Busy Days

Hawks hardly ever migrate at night or across the sea. The thermals they need usually occur only in the daytime and on land.

A hawks' resting place.

Airborne Caravans

Since most hawks follow the same flight paths south, there are only a few special places where thousands of them gather to rest. Sometimes, vultures, eagles, and even storks join the raptors to form huge flocks of hundreds of thousands of birds.

These spectacular convoys are enjoyed by thousands of bird watchers all over the world. Two of the best places to see migrating hawks in Canada in the fall are Hawk Cliff at St. Thomas, Ontario, and the Kananaskis Valley in Alberta. But there are other places right across the country where you can see one, or even a hundred, fly past.

One of the nice things about watching hawks migrate is that you don't need binoculars to see them fly. Call your local bird-watching or naturalist society and ask if there is a place not far from where you live to see migrating hawks. Then ask your parents to take you and your friends there for a picnic. While you're enjoying yourselves, look up, look way up, and see if you can spot this silhouette.

More Migrating Marvels

The smallest migratory bird is the ruby-throated hummingbird. From the tip of its long, pointy beak to the end of its tail feathers, this tiny flyer measures only nine centimetres and weighs about as much as two pennies. It will migrate from southern Canada to Florida or southern Mexico, beating its wings roughly fifty times per second all the way.

A ruby-throated hummingbird.

A golden eagle.

An arctic tern.

The arctic tern, which breeds in the arctic and migrates to Antarctica, holds the record for the farthest distance travelled each year: 17 700 kilometres from the North Pole to the South Pole and the same distance back again.

One of the largest migratory birds in Canada is the golden eagle, which weighs in at about five kilograms. With a wingspan of 2.3 metres, this raptor will flap and soar all the way to Central and South America.

Albert

The True Story of a Peregrine Falcon

by Marcy Cottrell Houle
Illustrated by Josée Morin

One chilly spring morning high in the mountains of Colorado, two small peregrine falcons were born. No soft feathers or grass lined their nest, or aerie. Their home was a hard ledge covered with dirt and small rocks near the top of a towering cliff. Frosty winds blew around the precipice, and snow glistened in the forested foothills below. Yet the peregrines were not uncomfortable. Their mother and father tended them carefully—feeding the nestlings when they were hungry and shielding them from the wind with their larger, soft bodies.

At first the two peregrines spent most of their time sleeping. Born blind and helpless, they could do little but eat. Yet soon long, tapering grey and white feathers replaced their soft downy ones. Their yellow feet grew large and strong. By the time they were only six weeks old, they were as big and handsome as their parents.

The two young peregrines, absorbed in their own affairs, were not aware that they were being watched. A wildlife biologist was studying them. For six weeks she had been writing down everything she saw them doing, for these birds were special. They belonged to a race known as *Falco peregrinus anatum*, the American peregrine falcon. Peregrine falcons are the fastest of all living creatures. They are also endangered, which means so few are left in the world that their species may not survive into the next century.

The young falcons did not know this, of course. Nor did they know that the biologist had named them Albert and Leopold for ease in her note taking. For the time being, only one thing was on the nestlings' minds: learning how to fly.

Unfortunately, this skill seemed to elude them. Especially Albert. Every time he tried to fly, his legs got in the way. When he ran along the cliff, he fell down. When he tried to climb the rocks to the ridge top, he slid backward on his rear. It seemed improbable that he would ever live up to the peregrine label "king of the air."

Leopold, however, was more adept. He could hop half a metre or so into the air and beat his wings so rapidly that he stayed airborne for several seconds.

Because Leopold could move so fast, he usually got first grab at the food, which was unfortunate for Albert. Then the day came when Leopold jumped off the ledge and actually flew. Albert watched as his brother pumped his wings wildly and zigzagged far above the ground, wailing a high-pitched *Ki! Ki! Ki!* Instantly Albert's father soared by and reached out with his talons to pass food to Leopold in midair.

Now Albert was starving, too, and he squealed for attention. But his father had already left. After an hour the adult peregrine returned carrying more food. He flew by Albert and dangled it in front of his son's beak. This was strange. Always before he'd dropped it off at Albert's feet. Albert screeched his annoyance. His father merely called out a soft *echup-chupp* and continued flying in front of him. Albert squealed louder. He was petrified.

The biologist, who was watching carefully, held her breath. She realized how important it was that the young peregrine learn to fly—and fly well. He was a hunter, and his skill at procuring food would make all the difference to his survival. At this point for his species, the success of each individual peregrine counted.

Albert ran back and forth. He jumped up and down, begging. But he would not fly. Finally his father gave up and deposited the meal at Albert's feet.

For several days Albert continued his stubborn resistance to learning how to fly. He preferred to go hungry rather than work for his dinner. Leopold's skill was increasing daily, but Albert's fear kept him from taking the plunge off the forty-five-metre cliff.

The biologist began to worry. She observed that Albert was getting less and less food. But there was nothing she could do. And then, one hot morning in July, Albert was not fed at all.

Leopold had left to soar on his own and explore the territory. The adult peregrines had not been seen since daybreak. At lunchtime Albert's father was at last spotted bringing home food for his timid offspring.

Albert, ravenous with hunger, was beside himself with excitement. He leaped into the air and, without thinking, jumped off the cliff. Finding himself in midair, he panicked. Floating down, down, down like a parachute, he crashed upon a rock halfway down the cliff. He tried desperately to grasp the boulder but slid backward.

Albert shrieked. He took off again and tried to hop and flutter back to the nest, but he didn't have the energy to climb the sheer cliff wall. High above him towered the aerie. Albert slid down to a level spot. He sat back and screeched for help.

Three hours later Albert was still screeching. In this unprotected spot, he was vulnerable to a wandering golden eagle or a great horned owl on the prowl for dinner. The biologist, hidden behind her blind, looked on with a heavy heart.

At last, when the sun began sinking in the sky, Leopold and his mother returned to the aerie. Albert jumped up and down and screeched for them to rescue him, but they could do nothing. Hungry and tired and alone, Albert rocked back and forth on his dark, narrow perch.

Soon afterward Albert's father returned to soar above the cliff. From his powerful talons dangled a tasty meal for his nestling.

Food! Albert stopped screeching. Suddenly he seemed to know that if he were to survive, he must learn how to fly—and fly *now*.

Giving his feathers a shake, Albert stood up straight. With Leopold crying from above, he leaped into the air. Wings flapping like electric beaters, he lifted himself higher and higher in furious fits and spurts, until at last he stumbled upon the aerie.

Quickly Albert's father soared over and dropped the food at his feet. Albert grabbed the morsel with his talons, puffed out his feathers, then dove into dinner. He paused only for a moment when he heard a strange sound coming from behind the blind. He didn't know or care that it was the biologist giving a shout of joy. All that mattered now was that he was no longer a nestling. Like his brother, Albert had at last become a fledgling.

The
Great Blue
Heron

Diary

by Elin Kelsey

Each year, great blue herons return to Stanley Park in Vancouver, British Columbia, to raise their families. Nearby, on the grounds of the Vancouver Aquarium, staff and visitors watch the herons through viewing scopes, then record what they've seen in one diary. Here's what they discovered!

January 17

The great blue herons have arrived! When I looked through the viewing scope, I saw three of them sitting in nests on the lower branches of the spruce trees, just beyond the Aquarium. At this time of year, it's rainy and cool but the herons don't seem to mind.

January 20

There are fifteen nests in the spruce trees—all ready to use from last year. Right now, two herons are fighting over one of the low nests. The plume feathers on their heads are sticking straight out and one is stabbing the other with its bill!

February 6

Until today, I couldn't tell if I was watching males or females. Then, I heard a heron expert, Dr. Rob Butler from the Canadian Wildlife Service, talk at the Aquarium. Rob said we've been watching just males. They return a month before the females to choose their nests.

February 19

This is the first time this year I've seen two birds in one nest who aren't fighting—maybe they're a male and a female! I guess we'll just have to wait and see if they stay together.

February 21

The female herons have definitely returned. I counted four pairs of herons, all in the nests that are lowest in the trees. Two birds are preening their partner's feathers. I looked in a bird guide and it said these herons are courting.

March 19

I think I saw one pair mating. One bird put its feet on the back of another and bit its neck. Then, it moved around a little, flew off, and returned with twigs, which the birds passed from beak to beak. This happened four times in a row.

March 24

An adult bald eagle landed in one of the nests and the herons had a fit! They took to the sky like a flock of pterodactyls. You could hear their squawks right down to the beach!

April 6

I watched a heron fly into a nest where another heron was already sitting. The one that was sitting got up and flew off. The new bird sat exactly where the first bird had been. They did this twice. There must be eggs in this nest!

April 18

Rob Butler, the heron expert, said the eggs should be hatching soon because it's been about thirty days since the first mating. Right now, there's a heron in a nest fiddling with something. When it looks down, it seems to cough. Rob says heron parents feed their babies partially digested fish this way. I wish we could see if this bird is feeding a chick.

April 19

It's funny—new things keep happening in the lower nests before the other nests. I wonder if the herons picked those ones first for a reason. The staff at the Aquarium are giving each nest its own number so the heron-watchers can see if the birds in the lower nests do better than the ones higher up.

April 30

There are two chicks in Nest #9, one of the upper nests, and one chick is really big! According to Rob, heron chicks hatch about a day apart. If there isn't enough food for them all, the biggest chick will push the rest aside and eat their share.

May 1

I saw a chick hanging over the side of Nest #9—dead maybe? When I went to look for it later, it was gone. I didn't see if it fell out or went back into the nest.

May 15

I can see chicks in seven nests. The two in Nest #5, one of the lower nests, are huge! They've grown almost as big as their parents in less than a month. Maybe the lower nests are the best places for raising chicks.

June 14

First flight! One chick jumped and sort of flew a giant's step between the branches. So many birds are testing their wings, the trees are shaking.

June 20

There is a difference between the upper and lower nests! We counted an average of two chicks per nest in the upper nests. Near the bottom, there are three chicks per nest. Maybe more chicks survive there because they're protected from the weather and eagle attacks.

June 24

Three young herons have left the spruce trees to perch on the roof of the Aquarium. From now on, they're on their own. Will they learn to hunt and fish well enough to survive? I'll be watching next January for the herons' return!

ABOUT THE AUTHOR

ELIN KELSEY

Elin Kelsey has worked as an exhibit developer and science educator for zoos, aquariums, and museums across Canada. She currently lives in Aylmer, Quebec. When she was a young girl, she loved to go on adventures with her dog "Slippers." At the end of the day she'd hurry home full of stories to share with her family. Her Grade 5 teacher encouraged her to write the stories down, and she's been going on adventures, sharing stories, and writing ever since. Elin says, "There are such amazing things to discover about animals, I hope the people who read my stories feel inspired to go exploring too!"

Sounds *and* Shadows

Illustrated by Mary Jane Gerber

The Bird of Night

by Randall Jarrell

A shadow is floating through the moonlight.
Its wings don't make a sound.
Its claws are long, its beak is bright.
Its eyes try all the corners of the night.

It calls and calls: all the air swells and heaves
And washes up and down like water.
The ear that listens to the owl believes
In death. The bat beneath the eaves,
The mouse beside the stone are still as death.
The owl's air washes them like water.
The owl goes back and forth inside the night,
And the night holds its breath.

Flight

by Lilian Moore

A hound sound
comes out of the sky

and there are the geese,
a ragged string
moving
heart and wing
        into the wind.

Flung back
unraveled
beating forward
re-knit
        in arrow flight

onward
without choice
to open water
from winter night.

A Family for Minerva

by Katherine McKeever

Every morning in spring, just as the sun comes up, the strangest sound is heard in our valley. A mother snowy owl is whistling and honking, and her three hungry babies are squealing for their dinners.

Hearing this commotion, the father owl flies to a log and picks up a big fat mouse. He flutters to the nest and dangles the mouse temptingly.

But *wait*. Something is wrong! The cries of baby snowy owls should only be heard in the arctic, not in a green and leafy valley. And owls don't grab mice off logs as easily as all that. The sad truth is that the parents of these fuzzy babies are not able to live in the arctic, let alone catch and kill mice for themselves. Both were shot and were so badly injured that they could never again survive the wild. Luckily, they were sent to our owl hospital, where more than a hundred owls come every year to be treated.

The mother arrived first, with her wing hanging down and blood all over her beautiful feathers. She must have been in pain, but she sat up bravely on a log on the front seat of the car. How astonished everyone was at the sight of a big white owl looking out of the window!

We had to take an x-ray to find out how badly she was hurt. Alas, her shoulder was smashed by three bullets and she would never fly again. I gazed down at her while the doctor cleaned and stitched her wounds. She was so gentle and beautiful that then and there I promised her that if she would get strong, we'd build her a lovely outdoor pen with a big pool and logs and stumps to perch on. And we'd plant a carpet of wildflowers to remind Minerva of the tundra.

Three times every day I went into her hospital cage to give her food and medicine. So that I wouldn't frighten her, I always bowed my head to her as owls do to each other. Then she stroked my hair to tell me I was her friend. Because I wanted to keep her trust, I was careful never to look her in the eye, for that would be very threatening.

As winter ended, Minerva was well enough to move outside and it was a lovely spring day when we put her in her new pen. She looked all around in amazement to see the trees and the sky! Then, with a fresh breeze ruffling her soft feathers, she climbed up on a stump. She looked just like a snowy owl in the arctic. But she was alone.

Two more springtimes came and went, and then one day a large box arrived. Inside was a pure white male snowy owl. At first he didn't seem badly hurt and we thought we could soon let him go. But even after a long year he was unable to fly farther than across a big cage.

When we realized he would have to be with us forever, we called him Mars and put him in with Minerva. They were friends right away.

Year after year we watched hopefully for signs that they were starting a family, but they seemed to remain just good friends. At last, the third spring, Minerva laid her first clutch of eggs in a nest on the ground. Thirty-three days later one owlet appeared! Then three days later another and, still later, another! Because they were hatched a few days apart, the babies were all different sizes. Minerva was always very careful that the youngest and smallest owlet got its share of the food, too.

How exciting it all was. Sometimes we could see little wobbly

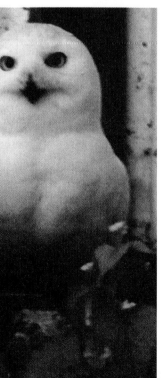

heads poking out from under Minerva's breast feathers.
And sometimes when the sun was shining we could see an
owlet lying out in front of Minerva on the warm ground. It
was wonderful to see how both parents knew just what to
do. Instinct told Minerva not to leave her babies alone and
to call Mars to bring the food to the nest instead.

Every time we put fat, dead mice on the food log,
Minerva sat bolt upright and started grunting and whistling.
This got the babies very excited and they squeaked and
trilled! What father owl could ignore a racket like that? Not
our Mars! When he arrived with a mouse, the babies
shrieked and tumbled over each other. How they loved to
eat, and soon they could each swallow a mouse whole.

By the time their downy coats had turned to solid grey, the owlets were waddling a few steps from the nest. Soon they would be spending their days hiding under low plants and flowers as they would have in the arctic. We seldom saw them, but their mother and father knew *exactly* where each baby was. And when I went into the cage to clean the pool or rake the gravel, Mars ran at me angrily. There was no way he would let me close to the places where his babies were hiding!

Gradually, the three fuzzy grey blobs began to turn into young snowy owls. Now, for the first time, we could see by their markings that we had two girls and a boy. And the two sisters were always pushing their little brother around and trying to steal his mouse. Often he would just sit by the pool, probably wishing he didn't have any sisters! Minerva seemed to understand that he was being bullied, so sometimes she would take him a special mouse and stand guard while he ate.

Of course, if they were in the arctic, our little owls would be starting to catch some of their own food by this time. And they would soon be drifting away from their parents. I felt that Minerva knew her babies should be moving out on their own, so I promised her we'd let them go free when they were ready. But first we had to move them to a new cage. It was so much bigger, they hardly knew what to do. One of the sisters found she could swoop up to a high perch. And then they were all flying all over the big cage.

Because they had to learn to hunt for themselves, we began to drop big, brown, frisky mice into their cage every day. How excited they were to see their food scampering around like that! Soon all three were chasing the mice, diving into the snow patches and the dried leaves. At first they didn't catch any, but after a few days they were coming up with mice dangling from their beaks every time.

At last they looked like true snowy owls with small, dark flecks on their beautiful white feathers. And what expert hunters they were—each owl had become fat and sleek. Now, with the snow melting, it was time to let Minerva's babies go free. We netted the young owls, put each one in a roomy box, and loaded them all in the car.

We headed for a lakeshore where dozens of snowies gathered to feed before flying north. The big moment had arrived. We opened the first box. Up, up into the bright sky went our first baby, her powerful wings taking her swiftly away. And then her brother soared after her, wheeling in the freedom of the sky. Then the last owl burst out of her box straight into the air, following the others. We watched them circle down into a green field to rest a moment. Then they took to the air again, and sailed on the wind as if they had always been free.

Our eyes brimmed with tears as we watched our lovely babies become three white specks in the distant sky. Then suddenly there were four specks . . . then five . . . then six! We danced with joy. Our babies were with wild snowy owls and surely they would follow them to the arctic breeding grounds. How could we be sad that they were gone from us forever when we had kept our promise to Minerva to set her babies free?

Our valley felt strangely still and empty when we returned home. But it only seemed that way. Minerva's favorite stump was losing its snow, and pink wildflowers were starting to carpet the ground. Yesterday Mars hopefully laid a mouse on Minerva's nest. Then he got up on a big log and honked defiantly at the whole world. Today, Minerva began to fuss around her nest making a hollow in the middle. And just a minute ago I heard the owls honking and barking a duet.

Minerva has babies on her mind again!

ABOUT THE AUTHOR — KATHERINE McKEEVER

Katherine and her husband, Larry, started The Owl Rehabilitation Research Foundation because they were worried about what was happening to wildlife around them and wanted to do something to help. They realized they couldn't help all kinds of animals, so they decided to dedicate their lives to helping just one kind: wild owls. Over the years, hundreds of owls have come to their Foundation from all over the continent and, after treatment, they've been able to return almost half of them to their original homes.

The Golden Eagle

One hot summer day while tanning and meditating, I thought that I should go to North America. I kept on thinking a lot about it and after a whole month I decided to go. On June sixth, I finally went to North America because I wanted to discover more about endangered species. When I got there I went exploring in valleys and mountains. While I was on a trip I saw a golden eagle. It was very large and was brownish gold. It was beautiful and I decided to take pictures of the eagle. I also videotaped the golden eagle as it was soaring through the sky.

When I returned home there was a lot of mail. One of the letters said that I could help support golden eagles if I raised money to help give them a better chance of living. I raised enough money in two weeks and sent it to the Golden Eagle Survival Committee. Two weeks later the committee sent me a letter saying that they used the money to help a golden eagle and its four babies survive and be returned to their natural environment.

Tene Carmichael
Grade 4/5

Henry

Once upon a time there was a blue jay named Henry. He woke up at the crack of dawn so he could get the fattest and juiciest worms before the other birds ate all the worms. All of his friends slept until seven o'clock. Most of Henry's friends called him "early bird." They thought that he was weird because he woke up so early.

One day another bird moved into the tree that Henry and his friends slept in. The new bird also woke up at the crack of dawn. One morning the two birds both found the same juicy, fat worm and they started to fight over it. They kept on arguing and arguing until all the other birds woke up. Then one of the other birds stole the worm that they were arguing over, and then Henry and the new bird decided to be friends and they never fought again.

Yael Leibovitch
Age 9

I chose to write about birds because they are pretty and I like the way they sing.

Yael Leibovitch

The Raven Letters

Sept. 11

Dear Aunt Margaret,

Yesterday I went for a walk in the forest. There were so many ravens! Guess what? As I walked towards my favorite tree, one of the ravens swooped down from the sky and landed at my feet. I've never seen a raven do that before. They must know me from all my walks in the woods.

I love you,
Caie

Sept. 13

Dear Aunt Margaret,

Something terrible has happened. The Housing Council of Wayeland Town has decided to cut down the Raven Forest to make room for more houses. The ravens' home will be destroyed! I've got a plan, though. I hope it works!

Your worried niece,
Caie

Sept. 16

Dear Aunt Margaret,

Success! My plan worked wonderfully. This is what I did: I made a sign that said "We live here too!!!" I carried this through Wayeland Town. (My parents carried signs too.) The most persuasive part, though, was that all the ravens were flying over my head. I think that scared the Council Head a bit! Now the woods practically belong to the ravens.

Happily yours,
Caie

P.S. So many animals lose their homes every day. We have to think of ways to stop that.

Caitlin Kopperson
Grade 6

The Blue and Yellow Macaw

Hi! I'm Eleni Vailas. I really like art and animals. My favorite subject is art. Now I'll just do a topic on a special bird. It's called the blue and yellow macaw.

This bird is not a meat eater, like hawks, eagles, and vultures. Macaws eat berries, fruits, nuts, seeds, and sometimes leaves. Some macaws such as the rainbow macaw are very colorful. These birds are peaceful, but are noisy. They have a curved beak, a black tongue, and they have big eyes. They live in jungles and rain forests. They are also very intelligent. Maybe a bird will hang upside down and then hang by its beak. Well, I hope you enjoyed my facts. Bye!
P.S. Thanks for reading!

Eleni Vailas
Age 9

Snowy Owl

The snowy owl has sharp bright eyes.
His feathers are white and fluffy.
His talons are sharp and shiny.
His eyes glow at night.
His throat will cast up pellets.
His nest is on the ground
of the Arctic tundra.

Kevin Reardon
Age 9

WINGS ON STRINGS

Kites and Kite Festivals Around the World

What aircraft is so efficient that anyone can fly it, and yet so simple that you can build it yourself? A kite, of course. All over the world, people love to fly these fragile wings on strings. Turn the page for more lore about kites

by Elma Schemenauer

A Little Kite History

Kites were invented in China more than 2000 years ago. They were made of silk or paper and bamboo, in many fantastic shapes. People flew them for fun, and also to mark special occasions. The Chinese also used them to send signals and to carry bridge cables across rivers. Other kites carried fireworks, and even people, into the air. A Chinese general once flew kites with bamboo hummers over his enemy's camp at night. The enemy soldiers believed that the weird screeches made by the kites meant they would be defeated, and they fled.

From China, kite-flying spread to Japan, Malaya, Thailand, India, and the islands of the Pacific Ocean. Everywhere they went, kites were a kind of magical link between people and the sky. Flying one was a way of sending a message from Earth to the heavens. This is the meaning behind many traditional festivals still held today.

However, new materials, designs, and uses for kites developed, too. For example, people on Banks Island, in Papua-New Guinea, made their kites out of twigs and braided leaves, and used them to carry fishing lines out to sea.

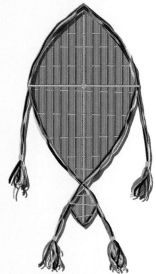

▲ *A Banks Island fishing kite.*

Kites came later to Europe, probably in the cargoes of trading ships that had visited the East. These first kites were flown just for fun. Later they were used for weather experiments. Scientists like Alexander Graham Bell and the Wright brothers used person-lifting kites in experiments that led to the invention of modern flying machines.

Today, all around the world, there are special festivals when kites take to the air.

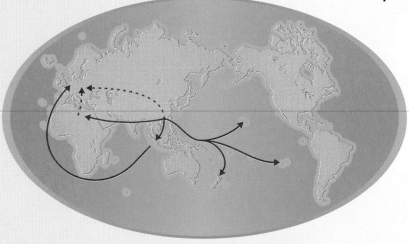

Kites were invented in China, and spread all around the world.

KODOMO-NO-HI

This Japanese festival used to be known as Boy's Day, but is now called Children's Day. In Japan, the carp fish is known for its courage and strength. On May 5 each year, families with children fly carp-shaped windsock kites called Koi Nabori on poles outside their houses. They are expressing the wish that their children may be courageous, lively, and healthy. Another traditional time for flying kites in Japan is to welcome the New Year.

▲ *Koi Nabori.*

CH'UNG-YANG

Many Chinese people celebrate an important kite festival from September 1 to 9 each year. It's called Ch'ung-yang, the Festival of Ascending on High. One possible reason for the date of this festival is that the winds that blow over much of China then are just right for kite flying. During the festival, children fly their kites every day after school. Some of the kites are shaped like fish, frogs, or butterflies. Others are shaped like centipedes or fearsome dragons. Many adults get together to build giant dragon kites that take five or six people to launch. On the last day of the festival, teams of people fly these giant kites from hilltops. At day's end, the children let their kites go, strings and all. Some people believe the kites carry bad luck off into the sky with them!

▲ *The head of a Chinese dragon kite.*

UTRAN

In India, January 14 is the date of a major kite festival called Utran. It celebrates the return of the sun and the lengthening of days after the short daylight hours of December. Millions of people travel to the city of Ahmedabad to stand on rooftops and fly their kites. Some do this as an offering to their sun god, Surya.

Kite fighting is an important part of this festival. Each kite has two lines. The regular line is for flying the kite. The other one is brightly colored, and coated with powdered glass. The point of the contest is to move a kite into position so that its sharp glass-coated line can rub against the line of another kite and cut it, releasing the kite into the sky.

▲ *A kite display in Ahmedabad, India.*

CHULA VS. PAKPAO

In Thailand, kite fighting is a professional sport. The most important competition takes place once a year in front of the Royal Palace in Bangkok. Teams compete, flying two kinds of kites—chulas and pakpaos. The star-shaped chulas are more than two metres tall. They have sharp barbs attached high on their cords to catch the pakpaos and pull them down. The diamond-shaped pakpaos are less than a metre long. They are easier to move about in the sky, and they have nooses to entangle the chulas and make them fall. Each chula that brings down a rival pakpao gets a certain number of points. Because the pakpaos are so much smaller, they get twice as many points for bringing down a chula. The winners of this competition become national heroes!

▲ *Chula and pakpao kites, Bangkok, Thailand.*

KITES FOR EASTER

In Greece, kites are flown forty days before Easter, on a day called Clean Monday. The most famous kite-flying spot is Philapapos Hill, right opposite the Acropolis. The kites are made in different geometric shapes, and are decorated with rectangles, stars, crosses, and triangles. Bermuda has an Easter kite festival too. It comes on Good Friday. People all over the island launch huge kites into the heavens to celebrate Easter.

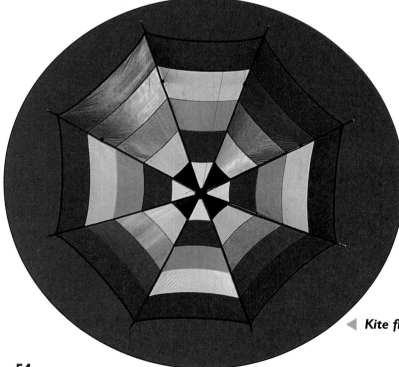

◄ *Kite flying in Bermuda.*

Famous kite competitions at Scheveningen, The Netherlands, and at Stuttgart, Germany, draw people from many different countries. These competitions feature stunt kites, which are built to perform tricks high in the air. There are new shapes of kites, too: the three-sided delta kite, and the foil kite, which is shaped like the wing of an aircraft. Often, kites are combined into huge, complicated structures called trains that take many people to launch. Some trains are made up with as many as 250 separate kites!

▲ *International Kite Festival at Scheveningen, The Netherlands.*

ONE SKY, ONE WORLD

A group of people in Denver, Colorado, has organized a world-wide kite-fly. Its purpose is to show that people care about peace and the environment. One Sky, One World is held on the second Sunday in October each year. All around the world, people fly kites on that day to demonstrate unity, peace, and goodwill. Every year, the number of people who take part in this festival grows. Today, more than 250 000 people in fourteen countries take part. People of all ages fly kites of every possible shape—from plain diamonds to cows and chili peppers!

A modern German kite with spinning balls. ▶

55

How Do Things Fly?

Illustrated by Renée Mansfield

Back in the eleventh century, a man called the Saracen of Constantinople decided to try to fly. He fitted wooden slats into a flowing robe and, flapping these makeshift wings, leaped from a high tower. His flight was a short one. It ended with a "splat!" on the ground below.

As time went on, would-be birdmen from all over Europe continued "hang-gliding" off castles and cathedrals. They all contacted the ground with the same rude jolt.

A few inventors had some success with hang-gliders in the nineteenth century.

But it wasn't really until the 1960s that hang-gliding caught on as a safe and popular sport.

Hang-gliders work the same way as all other flying things. They put air to work to help them fly. How? When a hang-glider throws himself off a cliff, air starts flowing around the glider's wing. The faster air moves, the lower the air pressure. The curved shape of the wing makes the air move faster over the top of the wing than over the bottom. This makes the air pressure lower over the top of the wing than under it. The result is *lift*.

Can you make a piece of paper *lift* without touching it? If you can, you'll have an idea of how hang-gliders (and other aircraft) stay up.

You'll need:
• **a piece of paper**

1. **Hold one edge of the paper between your thumb and your index finger, letting the rest of the paper droop over your other fingers, as in the drawing.**
2. **Now bring your mouth close to your thumb and blow hard over the top of the paper. What happens? You've created an essential ingredient of flight, lift.**

What's lift? Whenever an aircraft wing moves into the wind, it cuts the airflow in two. Instead of one *airstream*, there are now two, one flowing over the top of the wing, the other flowing under the wing. If the wing had been built with a curved top and a flat bottom, the airstream running over the top would follow a different path than the airstream passing under the bottom. This creates a difference in air pressure between top and bottom of the wing, and lift is the result.

By blowing over your piece of paper, you provided the airstream that lifted it.

Playing the Angles

Frisbees need a lift, too. That's why they're slightly curved on top, to break the airflow into different paths. But the curve on a frisbee isn't enough to take it far.

Your throw makes a difference.

Try throwing a frisbee parallel to the ground. Watch how high it goes and where it lands. Go back to your starting point and throw again, this time tilting the frisbee so the front edge is slightly higher than the back edge. Throw it with a tilt. What's different about its flight path? Can you find the angle of tilt that makes it go farthest?

Amazing Homemade Airplanes

Tired of the same old paper airplane designs? Try these two unusual flying wonders.

Straw Plane

You'll need:
- one strip of paper 1.5 cm x 9 cm long
- one strip of paper 2 cm x 12 cm long
- a regular-sized plastic straw
- cellophane tape

1. **Make a loop out of each strip of paper, overlapping the ends and taping them inside and outside the loop. The overlapped ends will form a pocket into which you can slip the straw.**
2. **Put one loop on each end of the straw by slipping the straw through the pockets you've made.**
3. **Experiment with the loops in different positions along the straw. Try it with the loops on the top and the bottom and take turns putting each loop at the front.**

Paper 12 cm

2 cm

1.5 cm

Paper 9 cm

21 cm Straw

How does it work?

Paper airplanes—even the odd-looking one you've just made—fly using the same principles as real airplanes. When they're moving, the shape and angle of their wings cause the air to move faster over the wing than under it. This reduces the pressure of the air above the wing, increases the pressure underneath the wing, and the plane is held up by the difference.

A real airplane must race down the runway to get the air moving fast enough past the wings to create enough difference in air pressure to lift it, and then must stay above a minimum speed while in the air. A helicopter, on the other hand, moves just its wings—the whirling rotors. This forces the air past them at a speed that's enough to lift it off the ground, or slow its descent.

Here's another paper airplane that works something like a helicopter.

Heli-paper

You'll need:
- **a piece of paper 25 cm x 5 cm**
- **a paper clip**

1. **Follow the pattern shown. Cut along the solid lines and then fold on the dotted lines.**
2. **Fold A forward and B backward. Fold C in and overlap it with D. When C and D are folded, fold upward at E.**
3. **Holding it with E towards the ground, lift your heli-paper above your head and drop it.**
4. **Try launching it from as high a place as possible.**
5. **Put a paper clip over the folded part at E. Then see if it changes the flight pattern.**

59

Nervous and excited, ten-year-old Jordan McKibben is definitely "pumped." He lives in Calgary, Alberta, the city nicknamed "the hot air balloon capital of Canada." So he's seen lots of hot air balloons swoosh across the sky. But today Jordan won't be watching from the ground....

Flying on Hot Air!

by Diane Bailey and Drew McKibben

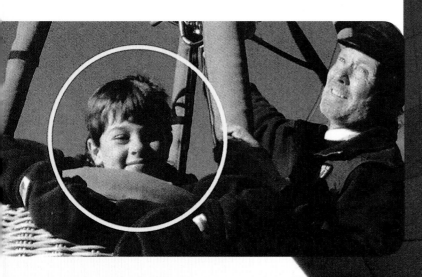

A Perfect Day

The morning is cool and calm. The "perfect conditions for takeoff," says aeronaut Dennis Myrthu. Dennis and two ground crew members get to work unpacking and assembling the hot air balloon. And Jordan gets in on the action, too. Jordan's first job is to launch a toy helium balloon, called a "piball." Dennis watches to see where the wind blows the piball. That's the same flight path he will follow. "You can't steer a balloon," says Dennis. "It goes with the wind." Dennis knows all about riding the wind. He's been flying hot air balloons for twenty years and he's flown all over the world.

Getting off the Ground

When all the parts of the balloon are laid out and connected, the crew uses a big fan to "inflate," or fill, the balloon's envelope with cold air. The balloon starts to bulge as it lies on the ground. Suddenly, Jordan hears a loud whoosh. Dennis has fired up the balloon's propane burners and he's shooting a bright orange flame—almost two metres long!—into the envelope. The envelope starts to rise. And once it's standing upright, everyone climbs aboard. The ground crew holds the basket steady until Dennis gives the word. Above the noise of the burners, Dennis shouts, "Let's go!" Whoa—*liftoff!*

Full of Hot Air

The ground falls away beneath Jordan's feet. The balloon's envelope weighs about ninety kilograms. Add the weight of the basket, three fuel tanks, a couple of passengers, an aeronaut, and how on Earth does the balloon ever get off the ground? Because it's full of hot air! The propane burners are attached to the balloon's metal basket. They shoot flames into the envelope, heating the air to a blistering 90°C. In fact, each burner gives off the same amount of heat as ten house furnaces! When air is heated it expands, or spreads out, making it lighter than the same amount of cool air. Because hot air is lighter, it rises—lifting the balloon high in the sky.

Hot Air Talk

aeronaut: a balloon pilot
basket: the part of the balloon where passengers ride (also called a gondola)
envelope: the part of the balloon that holds the hot air
mouth: the round opening at the bottom of the envelope
piball: stands for pilot-inflated ball. It's a toy helium balloon used to check wind speed and direction.
propane: fuel

Flying High

Dennis takes the balloon way up. To go up, he adds heat. To go down, he lets the air cool. Flight instruments help Dennis keep track of how high the balloon is, how fast it's moving up or down, and the temperature inside the envelope. Gauges on the fuel tanks tell him how much fuel he's burned. Flying 450 metres above the ground, Jordan gets a bird's-eye view. Through the patchwork of farmer's fields, the river winds its way to the horizon. Closer to the ground, deer and rabbits scurry through the bush. Fly on!

Splash and Dash

The wind blows the balloon across the sky, but Jordan doesn't feel the wind on his face. That's because the wind and the balloon are travelling together, at the same speed. The world is silent except for an occasional blast from the burner. Dennis keeps the balloon low as it floats toward the river. He wants to show Jordan one of the ways aeronauts test their flying skills — the "Splash and Dash." Dennis touches the balloon down on the surface of the river. Then he flies back up and splashes down again. After the third splash, Dennis doesn't dash. He lets the balloon float down river for a while. Whew!

Most balloon envelopes are made of ripstop nylon, a light and hard-to-tear fabric. Close to the flame, a special heat-and-fire resistant material is used that absorbs heat from the burner without burning up.

Up, Up, and Away

The hot air balloon is the world's first flying machine. But people weren't its first passengers. That honor goes to a duck, a rooster, and a sheep. This flying trio flew over Paris in 1783 in a balloon built by Joseph and Etienne Montgolfier. Two months later, the Montgolfier brothers took to the skies in a balloon made of paper and cloth. It was the first time that humans had flown. In 1785, a balloon flying from France to England burst into flames and crashed. This was the world's first air disaster. After that, hot air balloons became less popular. But in the 1960s, they made a comeback. Modern heaters and materials made them safer. Since then lots of people have discovered that ballooning is a real gas!

The Yahoo Landing

Dennis radios the ground crew to tell them where he'll land. It's their job to meet the balloon and bring it home. On a perfect landing, aeronauts can be very precise. But not today. The wind has picked up since takeoff. Dennis lets the air cool, giving it short bursts of heat so the balloon doesn't go down too fast. The basket hits the ground. Then it shoots up, bounces over a fence, skids across a deserted highway, and jolts to a stop. Since Dennis has let out the hot air, the envelope collapses, tipping the basket into a ditch. "That's what I call a yahoo landing," says Dennis. "That was fun," Jordan laughs. Not-so-perfect landings can be perfectly thrilling!

First Flight

by Catherine Friend
Illustrated by Richard Row

"Oh, what I wouldn't give to be up there, flyin' like that bird!" Charlyne lay in the dusty field, sparse patches of grass surrounding her. The ground was hard and rocky, but Charlyne didn't feel a thing as she stared up into the pale blue sky. A lone black raven soared above her.

Charlyne sighed and rolled to her feet. She couldn't fly like a bird and she'd never even seen one of those new airplanes she'd heard her pa talking about with Mr. Morgan. She was doomed to live with her feet always planted on the heavy soil.

"C'mon, Charlyne, let's get back into town." Her pa, the only blacksmith in town, had finished shoeing Mr. Morgan's four draft horses and was loading his tools into the pickup.

"Pa, tell me about those flying machines again, please?" As they bounced on the seat of the old truck, her pa told her the story she already knew by heart. "Well, it seems that Wilbur and Orville, the Wright brothers, who lived in Ohio, built this contraption called the *Flyer*. They tried to get it into the air for the first time—h'm, must have been nearly twenty-five years ago now—1903, I believe. It was a funny-looking thing, two long wings, one on top of the other, with a small platform for the pilot to lie on. Orville was the first to fly, and he kept that contraption up in the air for twelve whole seconds. . . ." Charlyne nestled against her father as he retold the familiar story all the way home.

The next day while Charlyne was helping her mother pick strawberries in the patch beside the barn, Charlyne's friend Hannah Ross came running down the road.

"Charlyne, Charlyne, did you hear about the barnstormer? Wiley Post is his name, and he's givin' free rides in that airplane of his!" Hannah paused to catch her breath. "The bakery's sponsoring him, so all you gotta do is give him ten bread wrappers from Chapman's Bakery and you get a free ride!"

Charlyne couldn't believe it. This was her chance to soar in the sky with the ravens and the eagles!

"Ma, can I take a ride, please?" Charlyne was frantic to fly.

"Well, I'm not sure if I like the idea of you being up in an airplane. We'll have to ask your pa. Besides, you know we can't afford store-bought bread. Where on earth are you going to get all those wrappers?"

"I've got an idea. Hannah, how long is this barnstormer gonna stay in town?"

"'Til noon tomorrow. He's usin' our pasture to fly from."

Tomorrow noon! That didn't leave Charlyne much time. As soon as she finished picking berries, she took off down the road to the nearest neighbors. "Mrs. Ashley, do you have any bread wrappers from Chapman's Bakery?"

"I've got one, honey. What do you need it for?" Charlyne quickly explained her plan. Soon she was heading down the road, the wrapper clutched in her hand.

All afternoon and evening, Charlyne went from neighbor to neighbor. It was well after nine o'clock when she dragged her tired body upstairs to bed. She figured she'd walked over fifteen kilometres. But as she fell asleep, she didn't feel her sore feet or aching back. All she could feel were the ten bread wrappers folded neatly under her pillow. Pa had said it was OK, and tomorrow she was going to fly.

Sunday dawned dark and cloudy. "Ma, do you think Mr. Post can fly in weather like this?" Charlyne worried as she finished her oatmeal.

Just then an automobile backfired out in the yard. It was Jason Willard from nearby Lexington. He called out to Charlyne's pa. "John, I got a horse that's lame, think it's the shoe."

While her pa got his things together, Charlyne told Mr. Willard she was going flying today.

"Well, Charlyne, if you're going up with that Wiley Post fella, you'd best get a move on. I heard he's leaving at ten o'clock to fly in a show over in Shawnee."

Charlyne was horrified. "Please, Mr. Willard, what time is it now?" Mr. Willard pulled out his pocket watch. "About nine-thirty." Without a word, Charlyne ran upstairs and got the bread wrappers, then hurried back down the stairs and out the door. She had three kilometres to go and only a few minutes to get there!

"I have to keep going, I have to fly," Charlyne kept saying over and over to herself, her bare feet racing over the dusty ground. She had to catch Mr. Post before he left!

Finally Charlyne could see the Rosses' silo, and she knew she was almost there. As she ran closer to the field, she saw Wiley Post's airplane. It was beautiful—shiny white with red stripes on the wings. But Mr. Post was getting into the plane, and people were waving goodbye.

"No!" she cried. "Don't go yet!" Charlyne reached the plane just as Mr. Post was putting his goggles on.

"Mr. Post, please," Charlyne was out of breath. "Please, could I have a ride? Here are my ten wrappers." Mr. Post looked at Charlyne's bright blue eyes and flushed face. He glanced at his watch, then at the wrappers wadded up in Charlyne's sweaty hand. He smiled.

"I need to take off for Shawnee, but you look like you've worked hard for this. Sure, I'll give you a ride."

Charlyne jumped up and down with excitement. Mr. Ross took her bread wrappers, then scooped her up and sat her down in the seat behind Wiley Post.

Mr. Post twisted around in his seat. "Here's your goggles, hon. Make sure you keep them on during the flight to protect your eyes from dirt. Hang on to this bar, and make sure you stay sitting the entire ride, OK?"

Charlyne nodded, too excited to speak. The propeller of the plane was

spinning and the engine began to roar as Mr. Post taxied to the end of the flat, dry field. Charlyne felt her body being pressed against the back of the seat as the plane went faster and faster. Her pigtails whipped the air behind her.

"Hold on, here we go!" Mr. Post shouted over the noise of the engine. And then it happened! The nose of the plane went up, and they were off the ground. Charlyne looked over the side of the plane to see the pasture below getting smaller and smaller. This was more wonderful than she had ever imagined!

As the plane levelled off, Charlyne gazed down at a miniature Mr. Ross, Mrs. Ross, and Hannah. She was amazed to see what her world looked like from the sky. The Canadian River curved around and around like a snake in the grass. She saw Mr. Ross's cattle looking up at the airplane as they grazed, and brilliant patches of green scattered across the blanket of dusty fields. She spotted a raven flying just off to the side of the plane. Now she knew what the raven saw.

They circled the area for five minutes. "I'm gonna have to make this a short ride," Wiley shouted over his shoulder. "Need to bring you down now."

As the ground got closer and closer, Charlyne's heart beat faster. Just when she thought they would hit the treetops below, they dropped into the field beyond. *Bump, bump, bump* went the plane as Mr. Post landed in the pasture.

Mr. Ross ran over, lifted Charlyne out, and set her gently on the ground.

"Thank you, Mr. Post," Charlyne shouted. "I'm never going to forget this ride, and someday I'm going to learn to fly an airplane just like you!"

Wiley Post smiled, waved, and taxied to the opposite end of the field. As he took off and flew over their heads, he dipped his wings from side to side. Charlyne knew he was waving at her.

When Charlyne Creger was in her early twenties, she realized her dream. She joined the Women Airforce Service Pilots (WASPs), an organization formed to train women pilots to fly military aircraft during World War II. The WASPs delivered new planes from the factories to military bases, tested new flying equipment, and pulled huge cloth targets that gunners practised shooting at. Charlyne learned to fly all types of military aircraft and graduated from the WASP training school, receiving her silver wings on 7 December 1944.

Plane Song

by Diane Siebert
Illustrated by
Pierre-Paul Pariseau

through the skyways
touched by clouds
over highways
over crowds
roaring
soaring
at full tilt
go birds that human hands have built

planes that fly
from small dirt strips
from runways on the decks of ships
from giant airports
busy
bright
hustling
bustling
day and night

planes of every shape and size
that taxi out
take off
and
rise
above a world of
tundras
trees
fields and farmlands
cities
seas
humming
coming
through the day
toward horizons far away
moving through the star-filled night
winking
blinking
into sight
high above us in the sky
hear their engines!
see them fly!

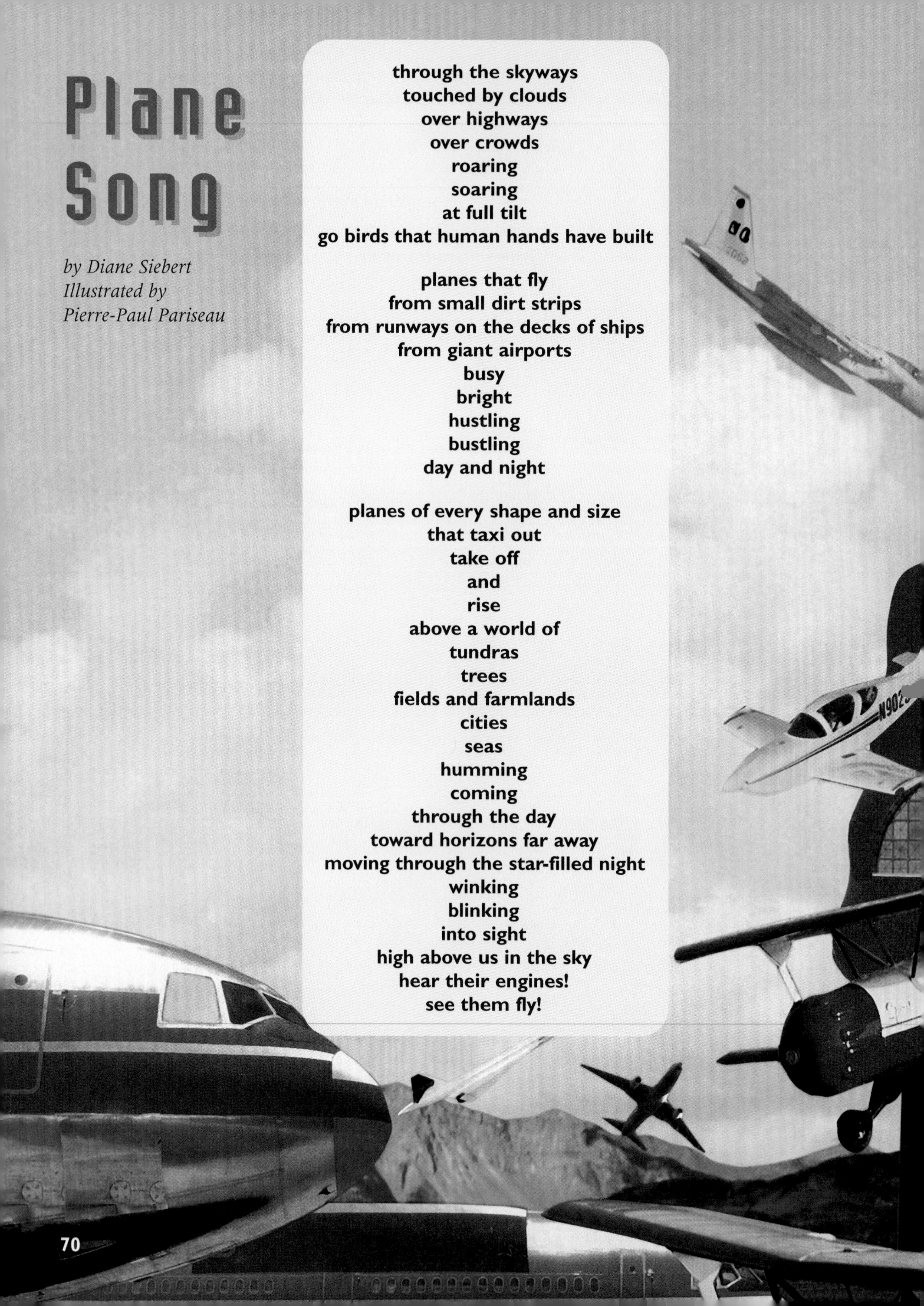

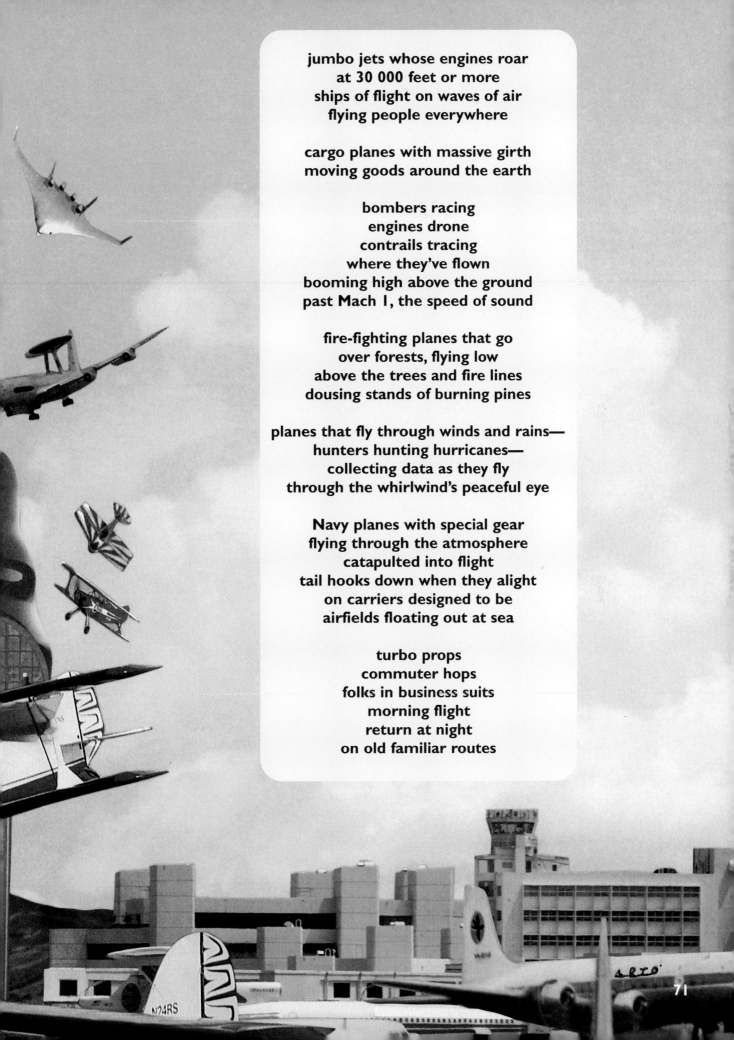

jumbo jets whose engines roar
at 30 000 feet or more
ships of flight on waves of air
flying people everywhere

cargo planes with massive girth
moving goods around the earth

bombers racing
engines drone
contrails tracing
where they've flown
booming high above the ground
past Mach 1, the speed of sound

fire-fighting planes that go
over forests, flying low
above the trees and fire lines
dousing stands of burning pines

planes that fly through winds and rains—
hunters hunting hurricanes—
collecting data as they fly
through the whirlwind's peaceful eye

Navy planes with special gear
flying through the atmosphere
catapulted into flight
tail hooks down when they alight
on carriers designed to be
airfields floating out at sea

turbo props
commuter hops
folks in business suits
morning flight
return at night
on old familiar routes

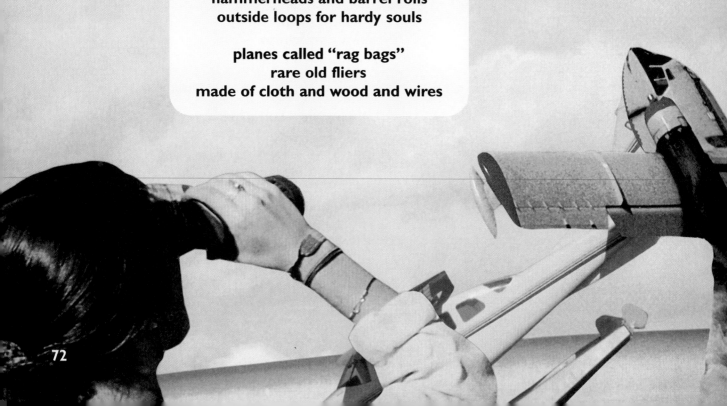

chase planes
pace planes
escorting outer-space planes
high planes
sly planes
picture-taking spy planes

bush planes braving wind and hail
winging
bringing
goods and mail
to places others cannot go—
islands, jungles, lands of snow
planes equipped with big pontoons
to land on lakes or on lagoons
planes equipped with giant skis
to land and stand on snow with ease

planes for writing in the air
advertising with a flair

planes for dusting farmers' crops
skimming just above the tops
of fruits and vegetables and grains
that grow on fertile hills and plains

quick planes
slick planes
doing-fancy-trick planes
aerobatics in the sky
stalls and spins done way up high
hammerheads and barrel rolls
outside loops for hardy souls

planes called "rag bags"
rare old fliers
made of cloth and wood and wires

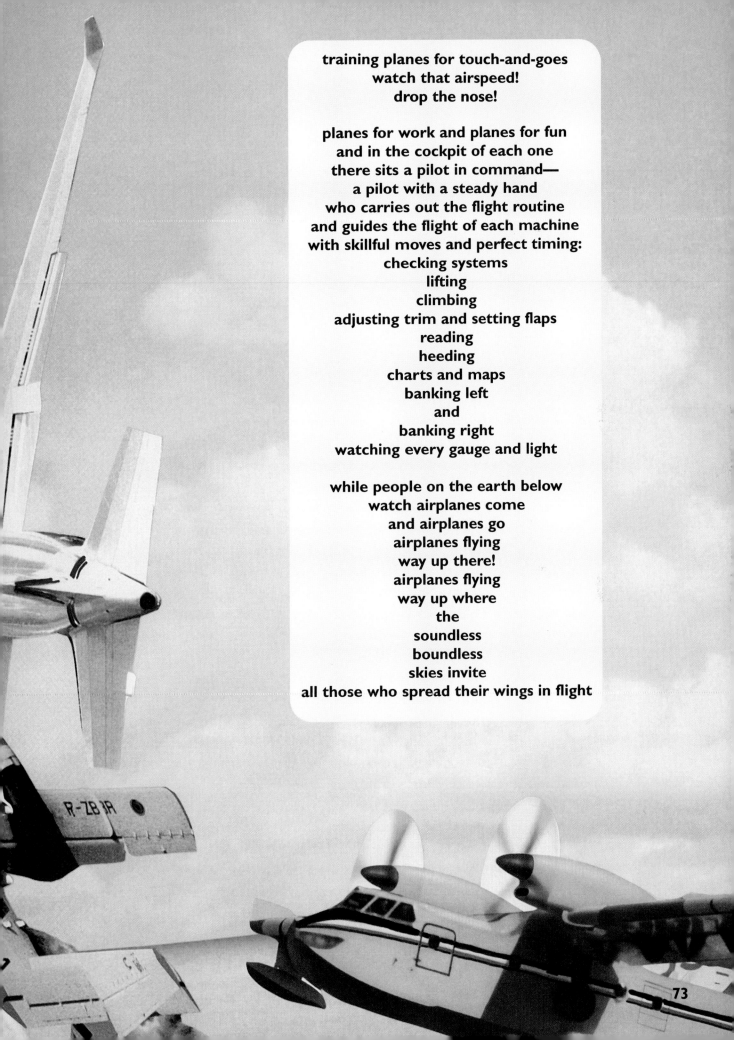

training planes for touch-and-goes
watch that airspeed!
drop the nose!

planes for work and planes for fun
and in the cockpit of each one
there sits a pilot in command—
a pilot with a steady hand
who carries out the flight routine
and guides the flight of each machine
with skillful moves and perfect timing:
checking systems
lifting
climbing
adjusting trim and setting flaps
reading
heeding
charts and maps
banking left
and
banking right
watching every gauge and light

while people on the earth below
watch airplanes come
and airplanes go
airplanes flying
way up there!
airplanes flying
way up where
the
soundless
boundless
skies invite
all those who spread their wings in flight

The Woodpecker
and
the Space Shuttle

by Daniel Cohen
Illustrated by Margot Thompson

The launch of the space shuttle *Discovery* was delayed for several weeks in the summer of 1995. The delay was not caused by some difficult technical problem. It was caused by a bunch of male woodpeckers showing off for their mates.

It seems that during the mating season the yellow-shafted flicker, a common woodpecker in eastern North America, has an odd courtship ritual. The male woodpeckers stake out their territory by making noise. With their strong beaks, they hammer on dead tree limbs. They even hammer on tin roofs. Their aim is to make a great deal of noise: the more noise they make, the more attractive the males are to the females.

Normally this behavior doesn't cause any trouble. But in late May, a group of woodpeckers at the Kennedy Space Center at Cape Canaveral, Florida, decided to take on something a lot bigger than a dead tree. They attacked the space shuttle *Discovery*, which was on the launch pad being readied for an early June launch.

The birds didn't hammer away at the metal skin of the vehicle or the rockets. Even if they had, they wouldn't have done any damage. The woodpeckers attacked a part of the fuel tank that is covered with orange-colored plastic foam. The foam, which is three to five centimetres thick, stops ice from forming on the tank when it is being filled with supercold fuels, liquid hydrogen, and liquid oxygen.

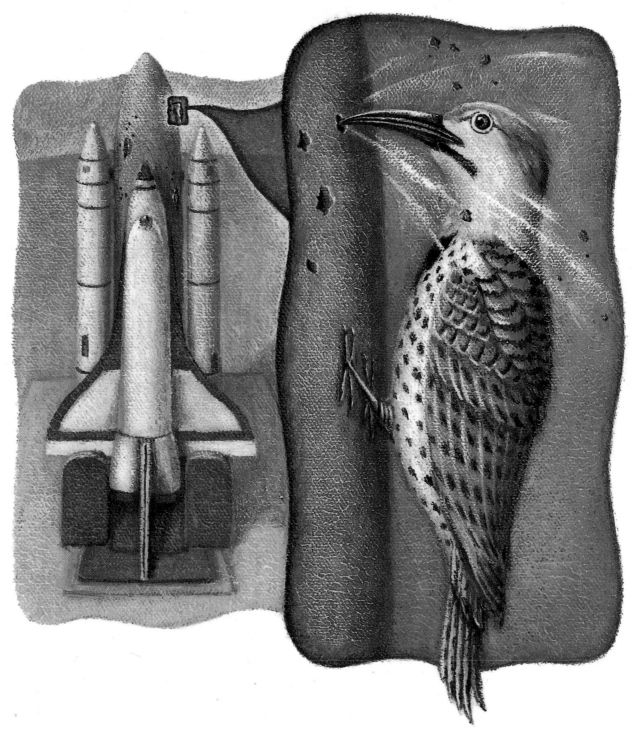

The birds pecked about six dozen holes in the insulation, some as big as ten centimetres across. In some cases, they hammered right through to the metal.

Engineers examined the holes and decided they had to be repaired before the shuttle could fly. The repairs were relatively easy. All they had to do was cut out the damaged foam and replace it with a new piece of foam. But the workers were unable to reach all of the damaged foam while the shuttle was on the launch pad. There was also a worry that the humidity would create problems in patching the foam. So the $2 billion shuttle, built to withstand the challenges of being blasted into space, had been stopped by a bunch of lovesick birds.

Once off the pad and back in the hangar, the repairs took only about a week to make. But then the shuttle *Discovery* ran into scheduling problems, which delayed the launch even more. There was no guess as to how much this delay would cost **NASA**.

NASA spokespersons tried not to sound too upset over the delay. "I consider this just one more rock in the road to success," said Al Sofage, the assistant launch director.

Could the problem happen again in the future? No one could say. The woodpeckers have always lived around the Kennedy Center. There had been minor problems in the past. But for some reason, the woodpeckers were more active than usual during the 1995 mating season.

In an attempt to protect the shuttle *Atlantis*, which was also on the launch pad, **NASA** technicians set up plastic models of owls and played recordings of owls hooting. Owls eat woodpeckers. That seemed to drive the yellow-shafted flickers away, at least for the moment.

No one knows if the woodpeckers will still be fooled by plastic owls and recorded hoots in the future.

Ride the Shuttle!

by Sharon Stewart
Illustrated by Dave McKay

What flying machine functions as a rocket, a spacecraft, and a glider too? Only one aircraft on Earth can do all that—the space shuttle orbiter.

External Fuel Tank

Solid Rocket Boosters

Orbiter

OMS Engines

Main Engines

The space shuttle assembly is ready to launch. The big orange fuel tank and the two rocket boosters will be dropped as the orbiter speeds toward space.

When most people think of the space shuttle, they think of an airplane-shaped flying machine. That's only one part of the space shuttle assembly that carries astronauts into space, though.

The orbiter is the plane-shaped part of the assembly. It's about as big as a passenger jet airliner. The orbiter has three main rocket engines that fire only during takeoff. It also has two smaller sets of engines used only in space. The Orbital Maneuvering System rockets (OMS engines) move the shuttle into and out of orbit. The Reaction Control System (RCS) engines are small jets that allow the pilot to move the shuttle around when it's in orbit.

The fuel for the orbiter's main engines is carried in the big orange fuel tank attached to the outside of the orbiter. The two rocket boosters attached to both sides of the orbiter carry solid fuel. These rockets fire at takeoff, providing most of the power that hurls the shuttle toward space.

Now it's minus 10 and counting. 3 . . . 2 . . . 1 . . . . Ignition!

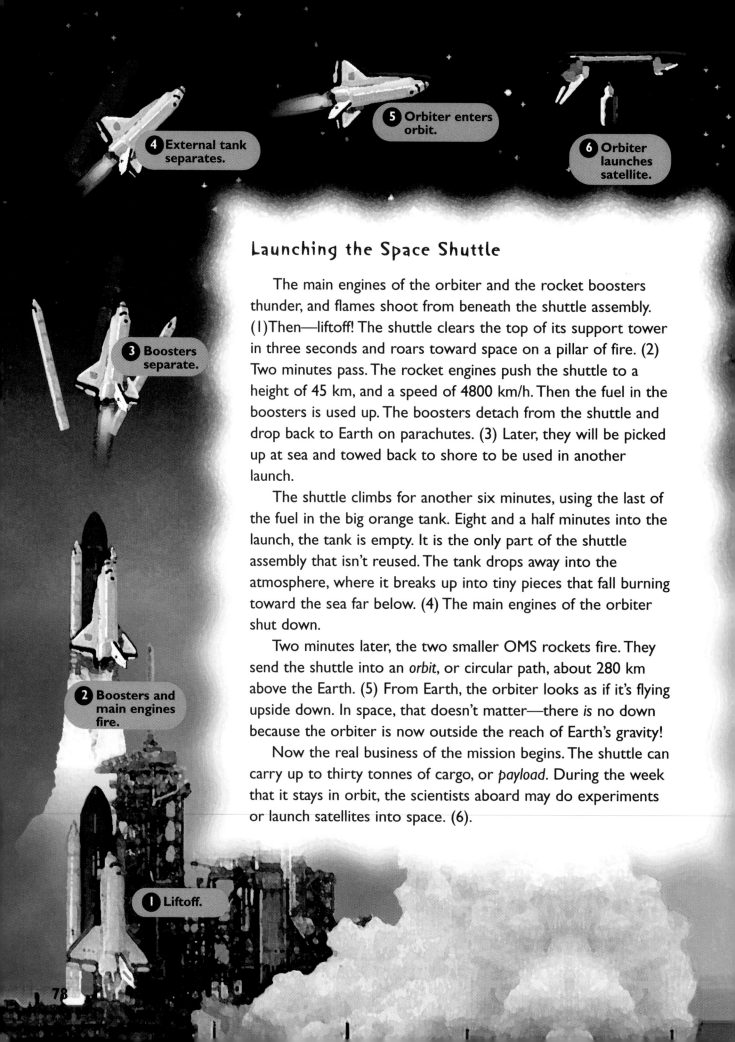

5 Orbiter enters orbit.

6 Orbiter launches satellite.

4 External tank separates.

3 Boosters separate.

2 Boosters and main engines fire.

1 Liftoff.

Launching the Space Shuttle

The main engines of the orbiter and the rocket boosters thunder, and flames shoot from beneath the shuttle assembly. (1) Then—liftoff! The shuttle clears the top of its support tower in three seconds and roars toward space on a pillar of fire. (2) Two minutes pass. The rocket engines push the shuttle to a height of 45 km, and a speed of 4800 km/h. Then the fuel in the boosters is used up. The boosters detach from the shuttle and drop back to Earth on parachutes. (3) Later, they will be picked up at sea and towed back to shore to be used in another launch.

The shuttle climbs for another six minutes, using the last of the fuel in the big orange tank. Eight and a half minutes into the launch, the tank is empty. It is the only part of the shuttle assembly that isn't reused. The tank drops away into the atmosphere, where it breaks up into tiny pieces that fall burning toward the sea far below. (4) The main engines of the orbiter shut down.

Two minutes later, the two smaller OMS rockets fire. They send the shuttle into an *orbit*, or circular path, about 280 km above the Earth. (5) From Earth, the orbiter looks as if it's flying upside down. In space, that doesn't matter—there *is* no down because the orbiter is now outside the reach of Earth's gravity!

Now the real business of the mission begins. The shuttle can carry up to thirty tonnes of cargo, or *payload*. During the week that it stays in orbit, the scientists aboard may do experiments or launch satellites into space. (6).

7 RSC burns.

8 De-orbit burn.

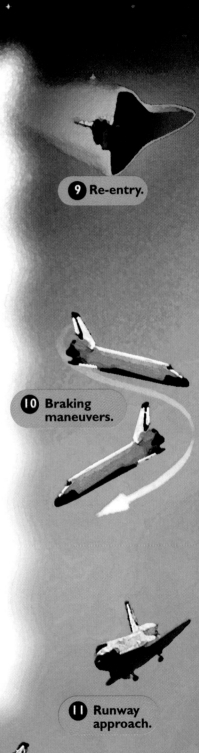

9 Re-entry.

10 Braking maneuvers.

11 Runway approach.

Re-entry

When it's time to return to Earth, the pilot uses the RCS jets to turn the orbiter around so that it's flying backwards. (7) After that, the OMS rockets fire again, slowing the shuttle so it begins to fall out of orbit. (8) Then the RCS jets turn the orbiter nose-up for re-entry.

About thirty minutes later, the orbiter plunges back into the Earth's upper atmosphere at 26 500 km/h. The rubbing, or *friction*, of the air against the speeding craft heats its underside to around 1650°C. The orbiter would melt if it weren't covered with heat-proof ceramic tiles made of a mixture of sand and clay. Though the nose and underside of the orbiter glow red-hot, the temperature inside stays normal. (9)

When the orbiter gets deeper in the atmosphere, it flies like a glider. The tail rudder acts as a speed brake. Flaps on the trailing edges of the orbiter's wings and under the rear engines change the craft's position. To slow down even more, the orbiter descends in long S-shaped curves through the atmosphere. (10)

Three minutes from landing, the runway approach begins. (11) The orbiter comes down ten times more steeply than a passenger jet, and much faster. It can only land on special extra-long runways. The runway approach must be correct the first time because at this stage the shuttle is a true glider. The small engines that move it in orbit cannot help it land! The shuttle's landing gear descends, and the rear wheels touch down, smoking. Then the nose wheel hits the ground with a thud. (12) A perfect landing, just an hour's flight from space. What a ride!

12 Touch down.

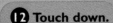

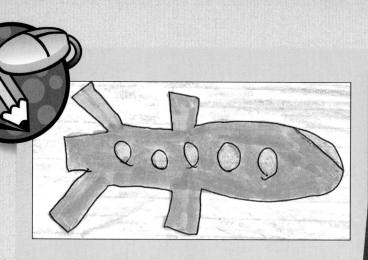

Greg's First Trip

The airplane is about to take off and Greg is excited. The airplane is lifting off the ground and Greg looks out the window and sees that everything looks like ants. Now they are travelling through a cloud and Greg sees what it looks like in a cloud.

It's lunch time now and everyone on the airplane is eating and drinking. Greg is surprised to find out that everyone gets their own tray of food and drinks. After they eat, everyone watches a movie called *Mighty Ducks Three*. They are landing now and the sign on the top says to put on their seat belts. Greg can not believe that they have arrived in Las Vegas. Greg says, "I'm going to love this trip and I hope we will go on many more airplane trips...they're fun!!"

Bryan Lampert
Age 9

The Kite That Saw the World

Just a normal average kid with nothing to do. Just sitting on a fence.

"Hey! What's this?" Joe asked as a bird flew by, dropping something on his knees.

"Cool! A kite!" he yelled happily.

Then he heard a voice. It said, "I'm not just any old kite, you know! I've seen places you've never imagined, not in your wildest dreams!" Joe was amazed at what he had heard and he didn't believe it.

"But now my journey has come to an end because I can't fly any more. I just went with the wind, but now I've finally landed, so I'm just another normal ordinary kite."

Heather Murphy
Age 11

Kites

The Bat Kite soars high into the evening sky
While the moonlight gently surrounds it.
It's a funny thing watching a bat take wing,
Especially when it's attached on a string.

Mr. Bat, Mr. Bat, how do you fly so high?
He rests his wings while the daylight sings
and soars with them when evening comes nigh.

Sarah Kemmers
Grade 5

Sarah Kemmers

I don't know how I started writing, but all I know is that I like playing with words. I kept playing with words until I started putting them together to rhyme. That's how I started my writing.